Dream World

D.M. Langdon

D.M. Langdon is also the author of

A Treatise on the Soul (2014)
Universal Wisdom for the Golden Age (2014)
Death Becomes You (2016)

To order further copies, please visit
www.vividpublishing.com.au/dreamworld

Copyright © 2017 D.M. Langdon
ISBN: 978-1-925590-68-5 (Second edition, January 2024)
Published by Vivid Publishing
P.O. Box 948, Fremantle
Western Australia 6959
www.vividpublishing.com.au

Cataloguing-in-Publication data available from the National Library
of Australia

Cover Design by James, GoOnWrite.com

Acknowledgements

*Sincere love and gratitude to my family,
friends and foes — we are all one
and the same, all teachers of the soul.
May peace be with you always.*

* * *

*I am eternally grateful to The Right Reverend
Jennifer M. Valls and The Most Reverend
Gordon L. McKenzie of The Light House
"The House of Light", for their love,
inspiration and guidance over many years.*

'The Book of the Dove is in your heart.
In truer form, knowest not.'

* * *

CONTENTS

1

My journey begins: personal messages of inspiration from my Spirit Guides

I have been channelling spiritual wisdom in written form since 2012, but I have been a Medium for much longer than that, with clairvoyant and clairaudient tendencies since I was a child.

Initially, I was astounded at the depth and beauty of the wisdom that came through to me when I commenced channelling. It triggered a deep memory, an understanding that this wisdom is not for me alone. It is my lifetime's purpose to share this wisdom with others. There are so many people suffering who would benefit from reading these simple truths and from understanding the purpose of their existence. This knowledge brings such peace, such freedom, how could I not share it?

The process is akin to meditation whereby I

connect to Spirit and the words flow at an unhurried pace as I handwrite the wisdom I receive. When I read back through my journals and my earlier published books, I see clearly the journey my writing has taken. Different styles of writing represent various Masters over time, all with their distinct form of expression, including beautiful poetry.

The sections in this chapter, and throughout this book, are not always in chronological order but I have tried to piece it all together in a way that is logical. This is particularly so of the wisdom from Jesus, which was usually a short passage received here or there and interspersed amongst other wisdom of the day — an interjection of the highest order!

I feel very honoured and privileged to be the Scribe of this wisdom. I understand fully that my life will never be the same, and it is a certainty that I will be held up to much ridicule and spite. My Spirit Guides have told me so. This is all part of my journey.

This chapter contains the personal inspiration I received from the Masters. This often came to me on days when I most needed a boost, a reminder of what I needed to do — a spiritual kick in the backside, so to speak. Initially, I was not sure whether to include these passages as I know that this chapter and the next, in particular, will draw the most negativity and ridicule. However, people need to know how our Spirit Guides inspire us, how they teach us and assuage our fears. They keep us on our paths and gently guide us to the post. That nagging doubt, that intuition, that instinct, that flash of inspiration — you too are being guided!

My conviction is strong, and my journey thus far has included overcoming fear, pride and doubt. Nonetheless, my greatest fear is not the ridicule and spite that will come my way. My greatest fear is the potential realisation, on my passing to Spirit, that I have deviated from my path and not completed my life's purpose. This is the real fear we all hold in the very depths of our being; the disquiet at our core. The fear of getting it wrong. A life unfulfilled.

—D.M. Langdon

* * *

Waste not, the writer of the soul, for you are not who you think you are. It is but an illusion of depth and space. Give not an eye for an eye; to lose the day is to gain spirit and fortitude. You are blessed with forebearance and strength, and wisdom in solitude. Use it — create a masterpiece! And the bell tolls for you.

* * *

Never before has mankind been so deprived of love, so deprived of all that is good and holy. The crosses burn, the heartache churns and the populace is weary. They come to you to hear the truth, the truth of all that is holy. The truth of their beginning and their journey back to God. Many times we called to you, 'Remember what you came for!' The time is closer still and you shall not be weary, for God will lift you up and say to thee, 'The work of one is a duty bound to God, a promise of the Ages, a contract set in stone'.

In the sandpit of time all will hear their calling to the work of God, and the tender, loving joy of Jesus Christ our Saviour as he watches your endeavours and brings the truth to set you free. Be careful what you wish for. The light that brightly shines, burns the fastest. A slow burn will see you home, your duty done, your light upon the horizon of mankind's soul.

Deliver unto all the messages of love, of hope and light for the future borne of man. For mankind is struggling, is heavy of heart, and loveless sorrow is the truth of their endeavours. Lift them up, turn them around, and they will be in gratitude of love to set them free.

The future awaits, the holy are gathered, and the dreams begin. The music in your heart is set to bursting; the crescendo of love and light and wisdom set to burst right through the day. It gathers you up and carries you forth; the task is a joy to behold. For you will see that all who know you see a truth that saves the day, a truth that is theirs for the asking, a truth to right all wrongs and save the world from sorrow — the truth of love for all.

* * *

To reach for the stars is a promise made to God, to sow the seeds of love and truth of knowing. Do you know the time is now to see what you are made of, to see the glory of your soul, the fruits of your endeavours and the cloak of mercy wrapped around your shoulders?

When the time is right, you'll understand the nature of your task, the tools to set you free and the hunger that belies your fruitful endeavours. To know this truth is to know your soul, and you will not be found wanting. You will gallop ahead to meet the glory of the day, the thunder in your heart a distant memory of the Ages.

Seek us out. Know this day that the light that blinds is the light to lead the way — the light of your redemption, the light of the powerful and just. Tune in to all that is holy. The Holy Land is but a hop, step and jump from your heart. It reaches in and shows you how you stumble. Light the fire of antiquity, leave your sorrow where you found it, for tomorrow is another day in the glory of your soul. Tomorrow is the way of hope, peace and glory.

Ignite the light that carries you to your rest, it will burn brightly as the day turns to night. The fireside beckons, the showdown begins. The temple of your soul is warm and welcoming. Remember what you came for! When all is said and done, there is no turning back from love. Love will save the day. Love will save the world from sorrow. Love will repair all, in sickness and in health.

The day has come to — duty bound — deliver the

lines of old. Deliver the truth to make all hearts sing. Deliver the Word of God. You will find it beckoning you in the temple of your heart. The truth is young and new again. It comes to you without a flicker of doubt, and you will feel it rising. Like a warm moon rising in the night, the truth will start flowing and you will not contain it.

Spread the Word, seek to heal and you will not be found wanting. For all your moons will rise as one, and the river of doubt will cease to flow as the sands of truth keep rising. Glory be, our Scribe du Jour. Accept this burden with ease and grace, and your heart will sing as the truth comes home to ground you. Home to all in fields of doubt, home to those who wander in and wonder why they came here. For you will see that all who sing God's harmony are the greatest gift of all — a gift of love, pure and tender to bring them to their knees, a gift of mercy, pure and true to tell them what they're made of — a light in the sky of humanity's wake to lead them to the shore.

Blessed be to God, for we know why we prosper. Be healed and be in peace, for tomorrow you will shine your light, and all will see the future — it is grand.

* * *

Lest we forget the story of the Dove to lighten hearts and purify minds; the glory is there to find. Find it, seek it, and you shall know true happiness. In the haze of clouds there is a knowing light. It rises pure and true. The honour of the day reaches out to grasp the wisdom, pure and flowing. Free to all who seek to know the purpose of their soul and the honour that awaits them. Many a moon and many a tide be spent in restless agony, for when one does not know the point of their existence, what is the point of it all?

The time to act is now; the time to whisper in the news to take you home. The *Holiness of One* is the truth to tell the world, to share all you know in the cacophony of life. The twists and the turns of no-man's land are set to send you to your knees. For you know why you stumble. You see the passing parade and you wonder why you go there; the fields of glory distant as you pass by.

Persevere, and the knowing and the wise will ease your pain — the pain a symptom of another day, so close and yet so far. It reaches out and closes in, but you will see that the mighty and the loving know just what to do — send more love, send it wide and it will surround your heart with joy. The pain will not last long.

Do you know what we see? We see a heart of joy and happiness and the truth to set you free. The truth will come at you at speed and surround you in your sleep. Go with the flow, harness the night, put pen to paper, the time is right. You will be astounded. The pages turn, and love is on your doorstep — love to save the day, love to ease the pain and help all children grow, love to reside by your side and turn the key of hope. For this is what you came for. This is the burden carried thus far; the light in the sky of antiquity to lead you to your home.

In loving haste we say to you, 'Do the deed, don't falter, persevere, and all will be as it should be'. All will come together now as the moonlight hits the sea. The day will dawn as children play and Mother Nature sings her song of glory. The cleansing tide will wash away the tears of future's past. The planet reels and all will be forgotten as the sleeping giant awakens. The roar will be heard throughout the land as Neptune lays its head on Holy Ground. This is the curse of the Ages.

Listen and be wise, for none so wise as those who see the future at their feet and know what they should do — send kind and loving thoughts to all the world. Send healing light and love to all who go there. Awash with flames, the night-sky seeks to send its burden home, westward to the heart of all its sorrow. The agony and the ecstasy of a task unfulfilled, a promise of the Ages. Go in peace and see what you are made of. Never before has the night-sky turned to stone. Never before have the stars failed to shine. Never before has mankind knelt before the hand of God in wonder and awe of the majesty of the night. All will be revealed. A hammer and a sickle show the way to Kingdom-come; the tools to set you free.

* * *

It is not a dress-rehearsal. It is the 'real-deal', the bargain with your soul. And bargain it is, because Adam and Eve, in long lost temerity and pride, forfeited their souls away. They sold their souls for knowledge; a bargain set in stone. Their journey through the Ages of Mankind is what you need to know. This is the legacy that becomes you, the legacy of the Ages, the right to earn your soul with knowledge, wisdom and love. A powerful combination to break the seal of old, to earn your soul with love, pure and simple, and good deeds to save the day. For when the truth comes calling, you will be ready, and you will remember. The truth will rain upon your shoulders and the light of God will shine upon your heart. You will be redeemed.

* * *

Follow your heart, and the stars will open up their wisdom and shower down upon you the means to set you free; free from all that riles you, free from wondering why you came. For each and every purpose is a reason, and all will come to pass, it has been decreed. You will wonder no more; you will deliver the truth to sit upon the doorstep of life waiting to be let in. This is your duty, the reason you came here.

The purpose of your life is to spread the Word of God, the sacred Word that tells us how to live and what it's all about — our life, our burdens, our souls and our pathway to the Lord. For when you deliver, the stars will whisper in the secrets of the universe and all will come to know it; the wisdom of the Ages, the burning book of righteousness that sits right on the shelf, burning brightly with the truth of your endeavours.

This is a task so humbling that you will find you know not where to turn when they all come out to find you. They hoist you up and ask you how you know this truth. They will humbly ask the way to true forgiveness of the soul and you will show them where to find it. You will help show them the way — the path of hope and glory for their soul. And when you deliver, you'll understand the righteous beauty of your task and the keys to set you free. For this is what you came for, and there is no turning back from love. Stand and deliver and the moon and the stars will keep full pace with the glory of the Word.

The time has come to lay your burdens down, to light the night-sky of remembrance. The glory of the day stands you in good stead. The journey thus far is a journey to be proud of — round the bend of hypocrisy's shadow and through the doorway of love, light and forgiveness.

* * *

Fear not, that the time is standing still and still no movement out at sea. A watched clock never sets. Reveal the terror at your heart. Reveal the pain that never ceases. Reveal all and you will be rewarded, for the night-sky shares your pain and harbours good intentions for your soul.

This is the truth of your being, the baggage at the foreshore of your existence washed up at lonely town with the flotsam and jetsam of life's long miseries. Release the cargo out to sea; purified and petrified it causes no pain or sorrow. Calmer waters abate, This is the way to serenity and peace. Arrest this truth — know it, feel it, be it. You are no longer the cargo carrier of sorrow borne of pain of betrayal; pain of 'auld lang syne' that clings and knows no other home, a pain so deep that you feel it in your bones.

This is what you must do — intention to heal, intention to love — and give a dance of joy, for all around the Angels sing, 'We'll carry your burdens home'. Set them free and all will be well with the world. The birds will sing a song of joy, for you know where your heart is. The dance of the true believers is a wondrous sight to see. All glory to you, our Scribe, for you have not been found wanting. You pave the way to hope and glory and the pathway is paved with gold. Believe in love, believe in hope, and all joy will meet you at the bend, the corner-stone of life.

* * *

For all the reasons of your heart, the light is here to stay. You sing the song of the true believers and take your place at the table of love. For you know the way and are halfway home. You yearn for the light and the light becomes you; the light of many moons and many suns and many journeys home to God.

For you know what you are seeking, you know what seeks you out, and you reside at the table of plenty as the merry-makers rejoice at all you have been and all you will become. Round and round, the journey is steep, the tide is high, but you know how to foster good intentions for your soul; the journey-master's daughter of the light.

* * *

All is as it should be. The majesty of light will carry you home and will lead you to sweet endeavours of the soul. The dance of the true believers is a wondrous tale to tell; a story filled with wonder and awe. When you have seen the light, become the light, nothing can stop your progress.

The pages turn, the candles burn, and all will be forgiven. Come into the parlour of joy and understanding and know that you are treasured and loved. You know the truth to set you free in the night-sky of your intentions. Dig deep, dig for gold and the words will come tumbling out as the marching band is preparing the way in goodness of the light — the merry band of brothers and sisters who will come to you in love. This is a joy to behold, a divine gift to cherish all your days, a stamp of the righteous, a blessing be to God. For you are one and you are many, and the many call your name and call right through the veil, 'Listen up, we understand your heartache, but deliver the Word and all will be revealed'.

* * *

Hallowed be thy name. The journey is beginning, and the crowd comes out to play. Rest assured we are in your heart, and you will not be found wanting. We will ease the day and surrender the night and all will be well, all is as it should be. For here you are at the pinnacle of time and no-one can stop you now. No-one knows the burden you have carried thus far, and all will be revealed. For you are a true believer; you never doubt the wisdom of the Word to set you free. You understand the future is upon you, and the role that you must play. Stand and deliver, the truth will out, and all will see the glory of the day.

* * *

The never-ending merry-go-round of love and hate and apathy is a ride we all must take, but you can get off anytime, the keys are in your heart. One by one the walls come down — the daylight set to dawning — and you know now that what you need is a chance to lose the yearning, the craving for all you desire. Peace is upon you; the Word is in your heart and you know what you must do — spread the Word of God. This is the way to your redemption; the truth to set you free.

* * *

The way of the true believers is honesty and might — the caravan of power in the corridor of pain.

This is what you need to know. Prepare thyself for the games will begin at speed and you will be thrust amongst the glories of the Ages. Be willing evermore to send out love and light to those who feel such pain. For this is what you came for, to save those souls who need to understand the choices they have made.

Every time you sing the song of empathy and love, the stars are bright, the love shines out and all will feel its gaze. All will know the future they create. All will know the destiny of mankind. Live in expectation of the day that truth is known, for all will know that — come what may — their future is assured.

The weight of glory is on your heart, but you will understand the future is bright and you must stand and deliver the truth to all. For none so blessed as those who understand the truth is at the table, ready to be served — the table of the true believers in the Honour Hall of might. This is your birthright, and none can stop the good tidings upon your doorstep. Step right up, the show will start and you will know your lines. Deliver the truth to set them free, for you understand what riles them. Take heart that you are on your way with the mission of the Ages.

* * *

It is not as you have known it. It is not a flight of fancy for the truth to set you free. It is hard work and perseverance of love, a serious endeavour for your soul. One by one the books are drawn; the Angels await the coming of the Ages. With sweetness and light, they sing the tune on holy ground to usher in a new day dawning — of justice, peace and love for all — a blessing for the world.

Few know the truth of your endeavours. Few understand the tasks that are presented for their journey to our Lord. But you know this truth and you do us proud, for you are a true believer and nothing can stop you now. It is as you have known it. It is as we have seen it, and it is as God allows it. Full glory to you, our Scribe, for you have seen the light and nothing will deter you from your quest to be the Scribe of God. The Honour Board erupts with light and all who see your name know that you are righteous and write the truth to set mankind free.

Never mind the pain you feel, just send it on its way. The day is young, so much to do, so much you need to say. Do not dally. Do not wonder why you feel such pain, the echo of your heart. Relegate it to 'lessons learned', a mere blip on your soul's journey to the light. For all will be revealed. In loving embrace we salute you, for you are a true believer and glory will be yours. Your message will stand the test of time, and many will prosper from the Word. They'll understand the way to live their life is through their heart centre, and they'll understand the purpose of their being, the truth of their creation.

Speak now; the day has come when truth will lead you home. Truth is the milestone of destiny, the signpost of love in the journey of your heart —

a hop, step and a jump to the glory of your soul. Do not dwell on old misery or hurts; you know this pain that riles you. You know the sorrow of old wounds and troubles. Let go, release old ties; the anger will not find you.

Be careful what you ask for; the lost time of summer is drawing to a close. The simple life is what you crave, all peace and solitude. The whirlwind begins, it knocks you around. There is much joy to be found in the fruit of your endeavours — the blissful harmony of ripening fruit collected by the masses — the joy of giving, the joy of surrendering to the truth, the joy of doing what you came for. The sunset clause of life is no impediment to the truth that sets you free. The sunset clause of life — the human life. The story that you write in the bookshop of your soul. The truthful joy of being.

—The Masters

* * *

2

Personal inspiration from Jesus

I received these beautiful and eloquent messages of inspiration from Jesus over the last year or so. Although I believed at the time that these messages were intended for me personally, I now recognise that the words are simply too beautiful not to share more widely, and that is indeed their true purpose.

Many messages of love and inspiration from Jesus are included throughout the pages of this book, as noted or italicised. I hope these words inspire you to do your best, make the most of your short time on planet Earth, and understand the greater purpose of your life. Read them with your heart, not your head, and they shall surely resonate.

None of us is perfect, but all are loved by Jesus and he is waiting for you to call his name. He will teach you how to love and how to recognise your purpose and be purposeful. Do not wonder what your life is all about. Know it, feel it, breathe it in the essence of your being. Be loving, purposeful and wise, have joy and forgive all others, and the beauty of your life will settle on your soul forever more. Do not delay. The time is now to grow your soul with love. God bless and God speed, my friend.

—D.M. Langdon

* * *

Abide by me in all that is holy, for I will comfort thee. I am the truth, the path, and the glory. The path is set, the knowledge found — the Knowledge Tree of life. It reaches down and lifts you up and you will feast anew. The burdens are lifted, the pain erased, and I am by your side. Forever go in peace to serve the Lord, the tender-hearted and merciful by your side.

They call to you; the time is now. In joyous beginnings they lift you up and you will see the history in the making, the chronicle of life, the merry-go-round of mankind's sojourn — the journey of his soul. For when all is said and done, this journey will complete you. Alone in the ashes of love's sweet surrender; a new day for the soul. This is what we are made of. This is the hardship to endure, the never-ending rollercoaster of life — the ups and downs, the loop-de-loops, the tension and the fear, the joy and the laughter of true surrender.

* * *

Woe betide the masses who seek your journey done. They understand not beauty, nor wisdom, of the Word to set them free. The Word of God is set right by your table. The Word of God is a tome for the Ages, a manual for the broken-hearted as they journey round the bend of their deliverance.

Come to me and lay your burdens down. The sweetness and sorrow will be with you always, but you will know that each and every lifetime your wisdom grows as your soul embraces all that you endure with fortitude and grace. The light within is a beacon of hope to all who follow in your footsteps.

Delight in all that greets you on the 'morrow. The tide will turn, and all will know the truth of your surrender. Believe in me, and when the seasons call your name you will be ready for the sweetness of the dawn and the tools to set you free from all that binds you. Go now, and forever call my name.

* * *

This is what you came for. This is who you are. Be humble in new beginnings and cherish the day. Cherish the light that finds you dear and the Word to spread around — the true believers' signpost, the tome of the Ages. For all the journeys known to man, this one is staid and true. Verily this has come to pass, and you will not be found wanting. You'll understand the journey you must take, and I will comfort thee. I'll reach down and caress you with light, a light so bright that all will see that you are guided thus. All will see the beauty that surrounds you. You journey to the great beyond where the music plays, and you will sing along in sweet harmony of your soul. For you are a true believer and nobody can deny it. I will cover you in glory and judicious be thy name, for when all is known, the truth will sit upon the shelf of antiquity. Blessed be to God.

* * *

The day is long, and you know where to find me. Call my name and I will comfort thee. I will cherish thee and show you how to prosper. Do good deeds and don't look back. Cherish thy name, and the heartbeat of surrender will carry you home — home to all who hold you dear — and the glory to be found in love's sweet surrender will bring you to your knees. For He is there waiting, and none so tried and true as those who take the hand of God and lead where they will follow. None so blessed as those who see the light shining bright in the wilderness and find their way home to God the Father. And Heaven and Earth are filled with His glory. Hallelujah.

* * *

Abide by me in the city of love and take your guard rails down, for when you know love there is no need to hide away your light. Your light will shine for all the world, and all will come to bear upon your soul. The gift to mankind is a wondrous thing and all will know good deeds. Speak to the masses, spread joy and light and wisdom proud, and you will be redeemed.

* * *

Verily, I say to you, let the light shine brightly in the recesses of your heart, and the day will dawn supreme. The love you send will bring you to your knees, for you are a true believer and all glory to you, our Scribe. Your good intentions take you where you want to be — right by my side — and my hand is forever more leading you home, home to God the Father on the journey of your life. For you will see that glory days are here again, and nobody will deny it. Take my hand, I cherish thee, and all will be revealed. Delight in all that comes your way. Believe what may, the wherewithal of love's true surrender is waiting right by your side. The Honour Board of love salutes you. Go in peace, you are redeemed. Hallelujah.

* * *

Abide by me in the starlight of your soul and I will carry you home. I'll lift you up and the journey has begun; the journey to the heart of man where you will see the future that resides there. Their hearts of stone will soften now and cherish the new day dawning. For they understand the future is now, and all must take responsibility for the future that surrounds them and the glory of the day in sweet surrender of the light.

This is your promise to God and glory be thy name, for you usher in the dawning of the greatest show on Earth — the glory of the Christ Light and the Choir of the Angels. All will be forgiven, all is known, all is as it should be — the dance of the dutiful, the journey of the wise, the chariot to take you home again and cover you with love.

Do not be afraid. Go the way of the humbled martyrs who led a weary dance. They loved God so and they were not found wanting. Take inspiration from your merry group of friends who lift you up when you are down and show you where your heart is. The way of hope and glory is in your heart. Open up and you will see the shadows of your soul and the goodness that resides there. This is the way of the Lord, hallelujah.

* * *

Hallelujah to the day of righteous living! Come sing in tune for the cast is here to guide you; the choir leads the way to happy-ever-after. Live in love, and the righteous bow to your endeavours. The time is now. True peace awaits and glory knows your name, for here you are at the precipice of time and I will lead you home. I'll comfort thee and take your hand and lead you to the choir. You know the verse, you sing in tune, and all will be revealed. This is the tune of surrender. This is the majesty of light and the means to make you whole.

Come to me and the stars will surround you. They gather in anticipation of the glory of the day, for they know the beauty that surrounds you. They know your heart and will guide you to the post. Do not give into loneliness and doubt. Be strong, and the light will shine forever more in the recesses of your heart. Go now, holy one. And the night-sky calls your name, hallelujah.

* * *

For each and every one of God's children on Earth, the skyline of surrender beckons on the horizon. Know it, feel it, breathe it. Do not resist the pull of love so tender in its warmth, for you are a true believer and can see the glory that awaits. Abide by me and the future will astound you. It will wrap you up in holiness and love, and a gentle guiding hand will be with you always. This is a promise made to God and no-one will deny it.

The love song of destiny is a fortune of the soul. It seeks to harness the truth of new beginnings, and all will be as it should be, on the never-ending merry-go-round of love's sweet surrender — where all go hand-in-hand with the heartache of old. Abide by me, and the sunset of your life will be in glorious union of the means to set you free from heartache and despair. Harness this truth; the coming of the Ages is a blessing for the world. Hallelujah.

* * *

This is the way to glory. Abide by me in the wonder-
land of time and I will lift the burden from your
shoulders. I'll carry your sorrows and comfort thee
in peace and serenity, for this is how you venture
forth and serve your soul with love. Your journey
is a blessing of the Ages. Ride by my side, and the
fortunes of the brave will carry you to your rest. For
when you deliver the Word of old, the glory will be
yours forever more. And the future calls your name,
hallelujah.

* * *

Believe in self, do the deed, and you'll not be found
wanting. The destiny is by your side. Come to me
and all that is holy. The fireside of surrender is where
you want to be — the storyteller's sojourn into the
great unknown. The Lark and the Angel seek you
proud; all glory to you, our Scribe. The destiny
awaits the true love calling. Be calm and true and
listen to your heart; the peace and solitude of one
true love. The wilderness awaits; the time is now.
The frozen plains of winter are a test of the soul — a
test to make you stronger, a test to lead you on your
way to glory in harness of the light.

Take heart that you have come this far, and you
have not been found wanting. Take heart that the
blossoms will bloom, the flowers will open and the
nectar divine. This is the way to God's glory. This is
the way to soothe your soul to rest. Divinity awaits,
for peace will settle and truth be out — the truth of

your beginnings and the homecoming of mankind. For all his travails, all his glories are not for naught — each life a hankering to the last, each life a study in motion of how to set your soul free, each life a test of true deliverance.

Write it well, it will become you.

—Jesus

3

Sleepwalkers

Never before has the time been so right for you to call my name. Never before has the night-sky yielded to see what you are made of. I will take your hand and show you that the way to God's Kingdom is through the heart centre. Journey to the heart of man and listen to the heartbeat of time as it rounds the bend of loneliness and ignorance of the one true God.

Pain and suffering are the common ills of mankind. Show them how to love, show them the Word and teach them the way to righteousness of being. For when you are righteous, God's love is magnified, and all can see the love that resides there. Go now, the heartache and pain is calling to you. Teach them how to love, teach them of love and light and holy days, and all will prosper as they step out from the fog of their existence.

—Jesus

* * *

The School of life is empty but for knowledge of the 'Word'.

When we are awake, we are asleep, oblivious to the truth of our beginning. The fog of our existence seeks to keep us ignorant of the truth to set us free — free from pain and longing, free from despair and heartache. To find this truth, we must awaken to Spirit. We must understand that our task is to be fully awake, living a righteous life. This is our lifeline to the truth of our existence — the knowledge of the Ages, the reason for our being, the purpose of our life. We go through life as if in slumber, not fully understanding our tasks, our purpose, our raison d'être.

When we sleep, we are awake, we commune with Spirit and receive the guidance we need, our Spirits free and supported by love — wondrous love from the Spirit realms. Our Guides and dear departed ones converse with the wisdom of the day to steer our course home. Of course, we rarely remember these events of the night, these liaisons of love, of wisdom, pure and simple. But have you never awoken with the solution to a pressing problem in the forefront of your mind? This is a blessing, a gift of love. Your subconscious is aware of these nocturnal events and will guide you to the post.

In ignorance and fear, we stumble through our lives not really understanding the point of it all, the purpose of all endeavours. We sense there is more to it, but cannot comprehend the unease, the weight, the reason for the loneliness. Of course, you are never alone, your Spirit Guides are with you always. But if you are not attuned to Spirit, you will feel alone — an island in the storm of life. You wonder, what is the pain that riles you? What is this feeling of being incomplete and that there is something missing from your life?

If you know God and feel God in your heart, then you are blessed beyond knowing, for you are halfway home and righteousness will be with you always. If you go to church and claim to know God, but act in selfishness and greed, hatred and loathing, then your pain is magnified, because you know the way and have taken the nearest exit, the detour off the path of love and good intentions and onto Hypocrite's Way, where the light dims and goodness is in short supply. What say you, when faced with choices on the path of life? You can go back anytime and stay true to your path.

Your subconscious mind is the go-between, the intermediary between you and your higher self. This is where your intuition comes into play. It is your ego which lets you believe you are all alone, an island, unique in that none could possibly understand you. You wear a mask to the world and hope that no-one will uncover your secrets. You *are* special of course — special in your uniqueness as a child of God — but you are not alone, you are never alone.

We are all the same, finding our way, stumbling down our pathways to our goals. The path of learning for our souls is where the tests come thick and fast, big and small, and the pain is buried deep — pain and disappointment, hurt and sorrow and non-forgiveness. In this you can be sure — we are all the same, but some are further down their paths than others, shedding their burdens as they go. Others collect more along the way, meandering off their path in many a circuitous motion. Others choose a different path, and their soul's journey is to teach others, to help others, and sometimes this involves great pain and suffering.

Know that where you are right now is progress for your soul. Do the best you can. Never compare yourself to others. Never wonder, 'Why?', only, 'Why not?' Be clear in your intentions and let nothing impede your progress. Round and round the wheel of life, the duty bound are steadfast in their endeavours to light the fire of glory for their soul. Up and down, round and round, how we all do weary in this school of life.

Do not delay. Set about reforming all aspects of your life that let you down, all aspects that cause you heartache, misery and shame. For that is your task on Earth, to purify and live from the heart centre each and every day. Be kind and know no sorrow — no hatred, greed or apathy to the suffering of all God's creatures. Look into the mirror of your soul and be proud of who you are. Be purposeful and wise, for you are loved dearly by Jesus Christ our Saviour. Cherish this truth and it will see you home.

Forgiveness goes a long way on the journey of

your soul. It will advance your cause, the cause of progress for your soul. It will give you a leg up, a propulsion of sorts, to navigate your path. You will be lighter, happier, and understand your true purpose — to forgive all who wrong you, and lay your burdens down. The burdens you carry on the highway of your soul, where each life's burdens accumulate; the frequent-flyer baggage at the Baggage Hall of Life.

Release your burdens. Forgive all, do good deeds, be kind and know no sorrow, and you will wake easy from your rest — light and carefree, no worries in the night. It will be more a celebration of your life to be had in the wee hours, when your physical body is sleeping and your Spirit communes with love with your Angels, Guides and Masters.

These nightly sojourns while you are sleeping are the key to your learning, your development, and your mastery of Spirit. *As is above, so is below.* We must in our lives become more like our Spirit selves, our higher selves. We must strive to be the best we can, at all times, to all people and to all God's creatures.

We receive such guidance when we sleep, such wisdom to behold, for we know what we must do when the dawn hits the window. We wake to the sense that we must be purposeful. We must acknowledge we are Spirit first and foremost — Spirit living a physical existence in the schoolyard of Earth — and we will learn our lessons well. Simple lessons of righteousness of being, of loving all others, forgiveness and joy. These are the secrets to behold, the purpose of our existence to grow our soul and take us closer to God the Father.

For when we are one, we are many. When we sing the tune of our surrender, we light the way to our redemption. Our many, many lives have led us to this point. And we remember. This is the beauty of the dawn. So when we are asleep, we are truly awake — awake to Spirit. And when we are awake, we are in slumber of the truth to set us free.

We slumber through life making wrong choices and not learning how to love. We have our blinkers on. We are blind to the true purpose of our lives and the lessons we have set, lessons planned before our incarnation. We are blind to what is holding us back — the hatred and non-forgiveness of another.

We are blind and do not see in the reality show of life. We search for meaning here and there and wonder why we do not prosper. We wonder why our materialistic lives are empty and devoid of meaning. All that glitters is not gold. Love is free, forgiveness is free, joy is free. These are the gifts to set you free, to awaken you from your life of slumber where sleepwalkers abound, not knowing what they came for and forgetting where their heart is.

Don't look back, look forwards with glee, for when you listen to your heart you can't go wrong. Your heart is the compass to lead the way to glory. Open up and feel the joy that surrounds you, then commune with love and you will never get lost. Love will show you the way. Love is all things to all people, the currency of life. Love is the bridge between this world and the next, the fabric of the universe. Love is the means to awaken you from your slumber, from your sleepwalk through life.

We are wallowing in despair, and none can see the destiny that becomes us. Tomorrow brings a day of calm, purposeful knowledge for your soul. Knowledge that belies the grandeur of your soul and the task to set you free from the emptiness of life, where knowledge of its purpose is relegated to a bargain bin of loneliness.

Take this knowledge, stow it deep, for you will need it on the 'morrow when the day's troubles start to set your heart to stone. And you will remember. The pain is magnified, as you've carried this burden far. The pain is in remembrance of previous lives you've carried this hurt, this sorrow, and this is your chance to dissolve this burden on your soul, to rid it completely and transmute it to love and light. What are you waiting for? The starlight of your soul will glow pure and bright at this honour in the making. Reach in, open your heart and the light will shine upon you in all your glory.

Think kind and loving thoughts, forgiveness and joy. Open up, radiate light and love, and all pain will be forgotten in the journey home to God. Your loving actions will be applauded in the Spirit realms. The Angels will sing your glories and you will feel a lightness of being that will steer your true course home. Sleepwalker no longer, but fully awakened to the truth of your existence.

Joy is in the beginning and the end, and everything in between. Do not waste your life waiting for the momentous. Live each and every moment in momentous glory of the day, each day a gift from God, each moment a glory to be had. Treasure your time on Earth, it will never be replicated. This life, this moment, this day — a non-stop shop on the journey of your soul.

Give into peace and serenity of your soul. Give into the majesty of all you've come to know, for God waits for no person; no-one can jump the queue. You must earn your stripes and you must practice what you preach. You must surrender to the light and let no-one come between you and your God. The hunger will ease, the pain will subside, and all is as it should be, for this is the way to victory of the soul. The soul keeps marching on, my friend, and over yonder is the starlight of perfection.

Our life is eternal. Of course, from our miniscule viewpoint on Planet Earth the thought of infinite life can be terrifying, but that is because we have limited understanding of the truth of our creation. We know we must live a righteous life. We know the terror of getting it wrong and not learning how to love. We know the discomfort that wakes us in the night — the grim understanding when we have detoured from our paths, and the pain and sorrow that seeks to settle on our souls.

Listen up. Do not worry over pettiness and the daily grind. Fashion the day to suit the wearer's glory and the desire to do good deeds and think pure thoughts. Understand the worries that befall you. Delight in all that comes your way. Do not despair that the day is long, and heartache seeks to rob your soul of kindness — the heartache that seeks to settle in and journey to the mire. Resist the urge to wallow in the graceless act of self-pity when, truth be known, you have so much to be thankful for.

This is life. This is how the many Masters settle their old scores. This is how you live and learn, progress to the light, and transmute all karma along the way. You've been here before. You know the path to take, to sit at the crossroads and wonder how you got there. Take your time, you have the chance to do good deeds and settle in the path of 'most resist-ance'— the path of compassion, kindness and love, not ridicule and spite.

Arrest the storm that carries you to your port, for none so blind that cannot see the lifeboats waiting. The lifeboats of love, joy and forgiveness to all are waiting in calmer waters, where the fishermen get to cast away their sins, their burdens of the night.

Close the door on dishonesty and hate and remember why you came here — to grow your soul with love and to live your life more fully than the last, with love the mainstay of your creation. For when you love, your vibration is raised, and joyous is the night. Fulfil the need. Give generously of your heart and all will prosper.

Jesus will meet you at the crossroad and take your hand, and lead you onwards and upwards on the journey to the light. For Jesus is the balm for the true believer. He lifts you up and you will see that Heaven helps those who are willing to put others before themselves, willing to go the extra mile to help the struggling masses, to journey to the dark to lead the others home. For that is the truth of your surrender — others before self, humility before pride, love before hate, joy before sorrow.

Round and round, up and down, the emotions keep on piling. But you should know that the higher you go, the wheel it keeps on turning, but the emotions are refined; lighter and lighter, higher and higher. Only good deeds, joyous love, care, compassion and forgiveness are what you need to wear, every day in every way — the armour of the righteous, the gown of the true believers, the honorific of the chosen. Believe in love, believe in glory, and tomorrow comes the dawn.

For what use the Knowledge Tree if you don't learn to climb it? What use wisdom if you don't get to share it? As the leaf falls from the tree, so too the Word of God is free to all. Such glory to be known.

* * *

Abide by me and I will reveal the sorrow at your doorstep. I will ease your burdens and the heartache of the day. Take the journey, live it through, and the wise and the brave will call to you ... This is the way to God's Kingdom ... This is where your heart is ... This is why you struggle when the journey rounds the bend and you know not where to find me. Take comfort in the knowledge I am in your heart, for you can find me anytime and I can lead you home. I am the way, the truth and the light to shine forever more in the recesses of your heart. For you know the way by now, and nothing will impede your progress as you step out from the mire.

—Jesus

4

Love is the glue of the universe

Come to me in glorious union of the light, and the way will be clear and on fortuitous ground. I'll soothe you and show you how to prosper. The way to hope and glory is to stay right by my side in the never-ending journey of your soul. For you are blessed to know the truth to set you free, the truth of the heart of mankind and the troubles they all bear. Listen to the bird song, it calls your name. It lifts you up and calls to thee, 'Have grace and mercy and your soul will prosper'. For when the night-sky erupts in glory of the day, the never-ending rendezvous with love's sweet surrender is set to take you home — home to God the Father who awaits on bended knee for the foot soldiers of the Ages to return to His loving embrace. Hallelujah.

—Jesus

* * *

The lesson is not how to love but how to make it count.

When Jesus spoke of wisdom, it was pure and true and clear. Love is the mainstay of all — the wisdom you must learn. It is child's play, no less. Simple truth for a complex world. So simple you should know it. So simple you should show it. Why is it so hard for mankind to love all? Love is not an enigma. It does not require years of practice alone in a cave or monastery, silent and austere. Love is multi-faceted — a splendour and a kindness.

A reckless abandon of love will see you far. In good times and bad, love will sustain you, nourish you and protect you. It is a double-coated protection from the ravages of life, for who are we to doubt that love will save the day? Who are we to deny God's grandeur in creation, the glue of the universe, the energetic moonbeam of love? Pristine, crystal clear — a jewel to be worn day in, day out, its shine illuminating a thousand hearts, its warmth the reason the universe exists. Take this thought, stow it deep, for the concept of love is a concept all must accept with open heart and soul and mind.

Share this truth around. It behoves you to make a stand against the inequity of life, inequity of a world so damaged by greed and thunder, hate and spite, that many cannot breathe for want of love. Many cannot understand the way to their redemption. They feel trapped in a horror of their own making, in a world with no hope, no love, no life-force worth dying for — no life worth living.

Desperate times, desperate measures, desperate fools who think materialism is the only God they need to help them on their way — the way to misery and heartache, loneliness and greed, and dissatisfaction with life's wondrous bounty. Blood money, blood ties, blood oath — for when Jupiter is rising, what's it all for? A day in the life of the merry jester who knows when he is forsaken. He knows the part he must play and understands its purpose to distract the great and the weary from the horror of their lives — the sorrow that devours, the misery of the Ages, the tomb that enshrines mankind forever seeking glory for his soul.

The shame of the broken-hearted when they realise, too late, the fortuitous journey of life was beyond their sight, out of reach, out of mind, out of fashion. Take heart, this is mankind's journey of the Ages, the journey back to God, and Free Will is the Master in disguise.

What use life if no-one sees the purpose of their endeavours? There is such joy to be found in knowing where you are headed and whence you came. The beginning that has no end — the hope, the healing, the joy of wisdom's realm. Spread the Word. Bring light to those who suffer from darkness at their heart, the dark that churns and wears them down until the thunder that erupts seeks to devour them whole. You know this truth, this pain, this dark, and seek sustenance for your soul.

Every time the pain erupts you can see it in their eyes — the loneliness, the terror, and the means to make them whole. There is more to life than meets the eye. They know this deep in their hearts but do not trust their inner voice. Society drip feeds them the wrong type of truth — the belief that goods will make them whole. Whole shelves of goods, houses, cars — nothing shall be denied. These are mere illusions and nothing can fill the space, the space that's waiting for love and light, good deeds and holy grace.

The truth of all is someplace else and they can't work it out. They search and search to no avail. They find no Holy Grail. They understand they've missed the mark and God knows how they've failed. Try as might, some cannot fathom the wisdom at their door. They chew it up and spit it out, yet they come back for more. Send love to all, know true self; your journey never ends.

Time is the energy of love. Time is on a precipice waiting for the day to succumb to love. In all the actions known to mankind, love will conquer all. Love is the here and now, the essence of life — the hereafter and the always was. Sing the praises of the Lord, for Master Time has served his purpose well.

Round and round the wheel of life, time is running on. It weaves and dives, it pauses and jumps; such athleticism to behold. It never deserts, it's duty bound and carries the load of mankind. In hateful scenes it disappears, never to be found. For love controls time, it feeds it so, it nourishes and protects.

For every beat of mankind's heart, time is galloping on. When love abounds, the heart slows down; the relaxed and joyful prosper. But speed it up with hate and spite and you'll find time is unreliable. The window to life is time's best friend; it sets the scene for love.

The essence of time is a lonely place to dwell. The essence of all matter — time — is a master of deception. Time seeks you out, then seeks you stranded all the while. The never-ending heartbeat of time is the mystery of the Ages. Time is a one-way street. It lifts you up then puts you down in great mastery of manoeuvres. In love's lost grandeur, time pauses while you listen, a never-ending reminder of the mortality of mankind. The body ages, the body, dies but the soul is never-ending. The memories of all time are imprinted forever more.

To sing the tune of time and love is to understand creation. Time can run a hundred yards then go back to the start. The finish line it beckons now — the beauty and the terror. Time is waiting, it marches on — then the relay, pass the baton! Set the scene for somewhere else, set the scene for love. Capture time for yourself and you can't get enough. For time is lonely, all the while it wonders where your heart is. Do the deed, send out love and you will be rewarded.

Surrender to the light, the love, the joy of all existence. The secret to life is love, pure and simple. That's all that is needed. Love is the balm of true surrender. Love will see it right. It is the journeyman's master, the counterpoint of all creation, the means to the end, the end to the means and everything in between. Live with love and your journey will be prosperous — prosperous of heart, prosperous of all that is holy. The Holy Grail is to surrender the key to your redemption. For what say you, when faced with fear and you don't know what to do? Well *love*, of course, and all will be well.

The day will come when all will see the writing on the wall. All will understand the purpose of their creation. Cleanse away the fear of 'auld lang syne' — the fear of ridicule, the fear of pain. Loosen all ties with those who let you down. Surrender now, and peace will wash away the tears that fall upon your pillow; the tears of heartache and want, fear and disappointment, loathing and frustration. For you know what riles you. Grab your life with both hands; loosen the ties to materialism and greed. Spread joy and love, forgiveness and wisdom to all you meet. For you are a child of God, and none so fortunate as those who take your hand and lead where they may follow.

Work towards your goals, balance the books and pray to God for understanding. Listen to your higher self, your intuition, and make choices you are proud of; choices to follow you home and sing a song of glory for your soul. For when you see what you have achieved, you will be astounded. Little acts of mercy, small acts of kindness, a smile here, a kind word there — all badges of honour to greet you on the other side, ribbons to wear with pride. So cover yourself with glory. Start now, don't delay, and you will rest easy on the 'morrow knowing you have done your best and have no regrets — no baggage of the broken-hearted, no barrow of burdens to push on through the wilderness, no excess luggage to land upon your doorstep to eternity.

Cleanse your soul and release your burdens. Release old hurts, forgive and let go. Find your heart; it may be buried deep within an armoury of sorts, in a strong-box to keep it safe. But safety is not what you need. You need a kind, loving, open heart. Not shuttered off, not closeted away where no-one can find it, where you yourself have forgotten where you hid it and have verily lost the key!

Open up your heart centre, give freely of love with no expectation of its return. Unconditional love — that means no conditions, no strings attached, no bargaining to be had, no tit for tat, just open, loving expressions of tenderness and compassion.

Jesus is tender, loving mercy. Come to him on holy ground and he will be by your side forever more. The holy ground is in your heart, and he is set there waiting. He comforts thee and tells you how to prosper, 'With love, joy and forgiveness to all'. These are the keys to your redemption, the recipe of life, the cards to trump all others, the lessons we all must learn.

* * *

Come to me in all your glory and I will provide the means to set you free; free from all that is worrying and tiresome, free from the horrors of the night and the day that seeks to rob your soul of joy. For when the night reaches down and takes the moon away, the stage will be set for all that becomes you — all the burdens laid to rest, all the troubles dissolved to dust — for love conquers all. Love is the mainstay of your creation.

—Jesus

* * *

Without love, the world does not make sense. Nothing can take the place of love. Nothing can fill the void. Without love, life has no meaning — life is dry, lustreless, devoid of warmth and compassion, painful, sorrowful and empty of life. Love is the greatest force in the universe. The day love dies and turns to stone is the day we cease to be, for we cannot survive in a world devoid of love.

No-one knows the meaning of their life without love to measure it by, for love is the equation that matters. Love is all there is. Fear and hatred, spite and ridicule, war and hostility are all like death to the soul. Jagged little shards of poison to atrophy, rot and destroy — poisonous baggage, no relief from the burdens of might.

How easily does mankind create the burdens of ill-will? How easily does mankind squander all they've gained in ill choices, free-will choices that cover them in mire? And what is the point of a life lived in pain and sorrow, with misery and shame the garment of choice?

Release the pain, release the sorrow and sing a day of glory for the soul. For when pain is released, love rushes in to save the day. Love rushes in to soothe all burdens on the soul and show you where you came from. Love begets love — begets love! Love is the journey from the heart to the outer reaches of the universe. It is the universal language of all. Love knows no boundaries; it will find a way. Love is stronger than hate, love is stronger than fear. Love is.

And when they come for you — and you will feel it in your bones — you will know the secret that surrounds you. You will understand the journey of your heart and soul, and that there is no turning back from love. The road is long, and many meander to and fro and wonder how they came to be, but love will meet them at the pass and show them where their heart is. Love conquers all. Round and round the wheel of life, love will turn the key. Love is the antidote. Love and forgiveness are the keys to the drycleaners of the soul.

For none can see the truth who can't be saved. None can remain untouched by love's sweet awakening.

* * *

Those who understand me will receive me. I will light the way to their deliverance. Reside in me, my thoughts, my heart. Seek solace in the wisdom that you are loved and precious, and no-one else can take your place. Delight in all that awaits you, for you have come so far in your journey of surrender, and love will take you home.

—Jesus

* * *

5

Forgiveness is the medicine of life

Justice is not for the faint hearted. Justice is for one and all to carry in their stead. Do not mistake justice for charity. Charity is blessed heart towards those in need of food, shelter, love, forgiveness and understanding. Justice is the power to deliver mercy in your stead — mercy to the heart of mankind as he wallows in the mire.

—Jesus

* * *

Forgiveness is the tally that counts the most, the trophy to be most rewarded, the best in show, the honour in the making. It will make your heart sing with pride at what you have achieved for the glory of your soul, the glory to be found in absolving your karmic burdens, turning away from misery and pain.

Forgiveness is the biggest test of love. It is easier to love than to forgive. Forgiveness is the pinnacle of love, the ultimate prize, the Everest of your soul, the bandwagon of choice come to take you home. Jump aboard, the joy you will feel when you realise your accomplishment is indescribable.

Forgiveness is the tool to make things right, the tool to rise above pettiness and hate, the tool to help you learn the way of Jesus Christ our Saviour, the Master who inspires us and leads our journey home. For he is all and one, he is the light that brightly shines the way and shows us how to prosper.

Jesus is the way, the truth and the hope of mankind who flounder in the wilderness. He is the journey master of the righteous on the path to glory. Jesus came to show the way, to provide wisdom, clear and true, and help us understand the pain that finds us — the pain that won't subside. The emptiness of knowing something is missing, but being unable to pinpoint the hollowness of life, the reason for unease and the materialism that weighs heavily.

Soon departed, we learn the score. Of course, how simple, how could we not know? We were looking in all the wrong places. The blind spot of life is hidden in plain sight! The secrets of the universe reside in our hearts, for that is the treasure chest of love.

Go into your heart centre and listen to the heartbeat of time guiding you to your post. The journey within will lead you to the pathway of surrender, where all paths lead to God. Meander where you will, but you will find that the light on yonder hill beckons and the light will carry you home — the pure, wondrous light of righteousness and glory. Glory to your soul, glory to the seekers of the light, for they have come a long way to taste the fruit of their deliverance.

Mankind does not understand the purpose of life, the tests of love, and the growth of the soul to everlasting glory. If they knew, no grudges would be held. There would be no festering, ranting, hate-filled sorrow to block out all the light. No poison to leach down into the earth and fill the world with spite. No swirling cloud of misery to gather at our brows, just peace and serenity — oh, what a wonderful world!

Forgiveness is a choice, nothing more, nothing less than a chance to make things right, a chance to wave away the pain that sets real-fast. The pain of being unloved, mistreated, feeling less-than-whole ... done over, ripped off, ridiculed and hurt ... tortured, maimed, families killed — all degrees of hardship for your soul. Forgiveness clears the slate — real forgiveness from the heart, not pithy words of bargaining for the right to hold superior ground. It is a real feast of delight for your soul, for your life was productive and your burdens shed, not carried over to the next life you lead. A lightness of load, of being ... *A sheep to the fold, fully shorn.*

Imagine that! A celebration of love when you pass to the light and realise that for all your endeavours, forgiveness was your greatest achievement in life. How simple, but so easy to be overlooked; easy to pack it away, bury the hurt and forget where you left it. One at a time the burdens resurface, gnawing away in your old age, sitting uneasily, pulling the heart strings, demanding one last go to set things right. Like a puppet master, the burdens attach and manifest in physical displays of might — an ache here, a soreness there, a malignancy gathering storm. And all the while, the baton is passed from one life to the next.

Believe what may, the hardest task of all is to forgive yourself. In windswept times you carried the load, so many carts to pull. Then life became civilised, barbarity waned, but still the burdens grew. With each life led you learned a lot, but disappointment reigned. For not stepping up, you judge yourself more harshly than others may. Each failure adds to the pile of burdens on the shelf, the long-lost sanctions of the night set to all but fade away.

Love conquers all. Round and round the wheel of life we go until we get it right. Mastery of the key of life is what we all must learn; mastery over material goods, mastery over regrets and pain, and mastery over our anger and hate which is where it all began.

It was ever so — the hate of the other, the jealousy and spite, the disconnection from our heart centres, the need to win, not lose. But we are all winners in this game of life, we all gain glory for our soul. No life is wasted — every life a trip to death's dark door, every life a lesson in sorrow and joy, love and hate, forgiveness and growth. Mankind must learn that forgiveness is the key. Forgive all others and forgive yourself. Forgiveness is the jewel in the crown of life.

Forgiveness is the hardest path to take, but the easiest road to follow when relieved of burdens, light and carefree — no load to weigh you down on your journey to the light. No baggage to be packed away, folded in, creased into crevices, absorbed by the heart, the soul, the mind. The fog of memory distorted by the distant rumblings of vengeful pain and wishful spite, distorting and taking hold in the ether of your being, grabbing and sticking and clawing fast, absorbed and breathing a life of its own.

Can you feel the sadness, oh so deep, so buried and so raw? Release this pain, go deeper still and find where you have stored it. A pain or illness decades on will perhaps give you a clue. Find the treasure, dig it up and be gentle, kind and true. If you know what you need to do, the intention will work for you — intention to heal, intention to forgive, to remove the pain at last.

The cloud of doom hanging overhead will need a healthy blast. Love is the cure — forgiveness and love — that's what you need to do. You know this, but stubborn pride prevents you taking part. You think you've done nothing wrong, so why should you begin? Well that, my friend, is what we call, 'Not putting out the bins'. Why would you wish to accumulate filth from rage and hate and spite? It doesn't make sense to store it up, to block out all the light.

Forgive and let loose, let it go, send love and healing light to those who caused you pain. And next time around you'll be free of karmic debt when the 'debt collector' comes to town. For that is how it works you know; you pay a hefty price. For all the hatred, pain and sorrow stored, it ricochets back with might. Back and forth, sorrow and pain, what tag team has begun? Stop the rot, send back love in a melody of song.

Jesus knew just what to do, he gave a helping hand. He told all others to forgive their enemies, as the circus wears them down. Every day new burdens grow and attach with might, expanding all the while. Good housekeeping means you dust them off, transmute to gold and find joy and happiness in your wake.

The key is to be found in the recesses of your heart. Seek it out, know true love, seek forgiveness of self and you will know God. For God is never-ending mercy and joy, God will lead you home in glory of the light and sweet surrender. You have the tools to set yourself free from the shackles that bind. Use them, do not delay. The past waits for no man, the future ever-present. The way to the heart is to sing a song of gratitude and forgiveness. Your soul will be in raptures.

Intend to love, intend to forgive and intend to love yourself. 'Intention' is a one-man show; no-one can take your place. No-one else can cleanse your soul. No-one can forgive all others by proxy. This is your duty, your raison d'être, and you must do it right. No use crying, 'Woe is me', no use crying foul, for every time you refuse to budge, the burden grows a tail. It creates a heavy, bothersome bag of misery — black and sour. You feel this weight, it drags you down, it slows your energy layer. Rein it in, stop it now, don't let it eat your heart. Free the beast, uncage it now, you'll need to be much stronger. 'Intention' is the way to go, *intend* to set things right.

Lose the mantle of pride and foreboding that stops you in your tracks — the holding on to anger of the past, the holding on to anger *at the pass*. Let it out, forgive and let go. The moon will wane another day to show what you are made of — the agony and the ecstasy of a life well lived, the hunger for more as you see the marching band prepare the way to glory, the glory of your soul.

When fools rush in and take all they can find, with no thought for others — no welcome to the band — there are heavy hearts and lonesome nights when all is said and done, and fortune sings a song of loneliness for their soul. This is the way to heartache and hardship, when the browbeating begins, 'Why, oh why, did I take all I could find, with no thought of others' pain? Why did I not help my fellow man?'

The selfishness and greed and spite erects a monument to mankind; a cursed, stubborn block of parsimonious guilt wedged between a rock and a hard place — the Rock of Ages and the school of life on Earth. It grows and grows and takes on all the darkness of the day and the sorrow of the night. It fills and fills; it groans and edges closer to the sorry state of man. So close the breath is foul; the dreaded decay and rot the sign of evil brewing. If only mankind knew the evil that does go there. If only mankind knew that the monster of the deep is set to roaming, set to claw its way and claim its prize, its victory of the Ages.

All our baggage, each of us, contributes to the pile. Some more than others. It is the 'excess duty' of your soul. The cause, of course, is hate and sorrow and non-forgiveness of the day. No-one knows just what's in store as Jupiter comes to play. Jupiter lets out a mighty roar, he takes mankind's beast on. He knows just what's in store for us and never is he wrong. Soothe the beast, set it free, demarcate the host! Does this make sense? It should my friends, the beast's attached with might. Each and every one of us contributes to the load.

The drama of the old and weary is that they have no place to hide. Memories secure, they know the thoughts that rankle them. Lives lived in misery — of hatred, fear and loathing. Do not be the strangler of your soul. Do not ignore the wearying signs that tell you where your heart is. Do not endeavour to shut out all thoughts of peace and harmony. Go with the flow, be wise and true, and be humble in the might of majesty's calling. The past waits for no man; the present ever so. Do the deeds that rouse you from your slumber. The *might of one* is set to take the stage.

When you are young you forgive a lot, your heart is open and true. Then as you age, the walls come up, the heart closes in and forgiveness is an effort to be proud of. Believe in forgiveness, try it out, wear the clothes of strength and humility — strength to send all love around, humility to understand God's greater plan.

When someone wrongs you, stand your ground. Don't be a constant doormat, but forgive them in your heart of hearts and you will be much lighter. Lighter with no burdens to weigh you down, no karma to be carried through the Ages. Lighter as you live your life and await the final score. For you know the meaning of life, the simple truth of all — to love all others and love your God, and forgive all who wrong you. The simple recipe for a life well lived. So simple you should know it!

Sing the tune, sing it loud, start a mighty choir. The band, of course, is somewhere else but you can hear them if you try. All of Heaven knows the score, they want to hold your hand. To watch the future as it unfolds, to see who makes the grade.

The way to true forgiveness is the journey home to God. Forgiveness is the nectar of life, the balm for your soul, the precious jewel in the crown of your existence. For forgiveness takes you closer to God, closer to all you've ever been, ever was, ever will be.

Forgive, and your heart opens up a floodway to your soul. Forgiveness is the medicine of life, the lifeblood of all that is good and holy — a gracious,

loving cul-de-sac of righteous living, the culmina-
tion of karmic intention, the end point of hate, spite
and sorrow. It is the closing of the trap that keeps
us falling, keeps us failing on our mission back to
God. For every time we fail the test of forgiveness,
our burdens grow.

Forgiveness is honour in the making, a test of
true deliverance, full maturity of the ego, full bloom
of all that is holy and righteous and the reason that
we prosper. For what say you when, round again,
the wheel of life keeps turning, and you cannot lose
the hate and spite that keeps you empty as a sigh —
forlorn and sorrowful, empty of love, of life, of joy
and compassion?

Hold a mirror to your soul, what is it you see?
Pain and regrets, or pride and joy? What reflec-
tion is your goal? This is the way to God's glory.
Have mercy on your soul by paving the way with
best intentions of the heart. Live through the heart
centre, open up like a flower in bloom and watch
your heart unfold. The joy and beauty will astound
you. The birds know this truth. The birdsong of
summer will make your heart glad to be alive and
will show the way to live with best intentions of the
day. Sing now, and know that you will prosper.

* * *

*Believe in me and the wonders of life will be revealed
in all their glory. For what use life if you know not
how to prosper? Come into the parlour of love and*

understanding and the truth to set you free; free from the pain of old that grips you in the night, free from the ravages of old that seek to settle once more and burden your soul with sorrow.

Abide by me in all that you say and do. The stars upon their holy path will show you why you prosper. Believe in me and I will ride the night-sky of glory for your soul. For when all is said and done, the never-ending journey of your soul is a ride that each must take with grace and fortitude and gratitude of the light to lead the way.

—Jesus

6

The karma we all bear

The game of life is drawn. The proof is in the cards we're dealt when Karma does the draw.

* * *

Karma sets the tune for our deliverance. Karma is all things to all people — the speed humps of life, the chance to make amends, the choice to do what's right. In all our lives we carry our burdens forwards. Our tests provide a chance to clear the slate, to empty the drawer, to relieve ourselves of the burdens of the night. For many a lifetime's burdens end up piled upon the shelf of good intentions, gathering dust until our righteousness prevails.

The tests keep coming, the meter keeps running, so what are we to do? Simple — forgive and let go. Send love to all that pains you and live in joyous understanding of this truth to set you free. For karma is the beast of burden that helps to make things right. Karma is the greatest balancing act of love.

Heaven helps those who journey onwards to the light, those who tackle the tests and stride purposefully to their goals. For that is the path to glory, the 'best in show', the role model for all; it is the never-ending story of our soul. Believe in love, believe in all you aim to do, for we are each here for a purpose and the journey is just beginning.

The lesson of life is simple; you are what you become. Many do not understand the truth of their existence. Many do not wish to know the truth to set them free. Listen to your heart. Listen to your intuition, your instinct, and hear Jesus in your heart.

How do we climb out of despair and sorrow, when burdens are heavy, and no-one seems to understand our pain? How do we carry on shouldering the hurt and non-forgiveness? The Christ Light will see us through the dark days of our soul. The light will guide us to our rest. All glory to those who persevere, who shoulder the pain and work to release it. They understand their state of being and that the time is now to release and let go, forgive and move on.

All will be well if you understand the fruits of your endeavours, the karmic burden and the purpose of your life. Do not despair of all that riles you. Be tempted not, to act in graceless fury. Be kind and loving, patient as the day is long, and seek sweet surrender of the truth to set you free. This is the journey each must go through, and all will find the light and the pathway of glory for their soul. *The fortune of the brave is the dance of righteous glory for their soul.*

Destiny is a slow ride to eternity. Destiny is the peak of all perfection. Destiny is the cartwheel of joy in the carnival of time. This is the burden all must face — the burden of perfection. The burden of lessons learned and the majesty of a never-ending tomorrow. Be careful how you go there. The trumpets blare, the fanfare plays, but all must see the truth of their surrender, the truth of their beginning and the price they had to pay.

Karma sits right on the shelf, ready to be served. It bides its time — your legacy, your debt collector's card. For all the times you jumped the queue and waited by the door, your karma followed patiently, ready to even the score.

Grow your soul with love and all else will fall into place. Your troubles will fade away as you operate only from your heart centre. It is all about how you respond to those burdens that wake you in the night. Respond with love and forgiveness always, and you will be comforted that you are righteous of being and nothing can harm your soul. You are protected by love and God's mercy is divine.

Love is the armour of the righteous. Nothing can hurt your soul unless you allow it to. Jesus is the supreme example of love in action. He gave love so that we could follow in his footsteps and understand how to live, to feel the glory of the Christ Light.

Every day, in every way, the light will comfort thee. It will soothe you and take you home to God the Father in all His glory, home to where the heart belongs. This is the journey of the Ages, the road to your redemption, the glory seekers' pathway to the Lord. This is justice in action, redemption of the broken-hearted, the passage of the pure. For when the burdens are lifted, hallowed be thy name.

What's in a name? Who are you? Who have you been? What is the total sum of your existence, your many lives on this planet and other realms? Do you have an inkling? Be proud that you are here, and you are who you are — evolved and alert to opportunities of the soul, opportunities to learn in this school of life on planet Earth. The bell rings, the Masters await to share all they know. Take this wisdom gladly, take it kindly and take it wisely, for all you know will speed your journey home. This is the journey of surrender to surpass all journeys of the mind.

Do not despair the truth of it, you understand the way. The journey of your heart and soul is a ride we all must take. Never before has mankind been so ready to make the change, never before has seren- dipity paved the way with so much grace. Become a shining light, and the principles of light and love, hope and joy, and all things in between, will keep you on your way. Do not falter, stay grounded, and keep your journey homeward bound.

Forgive like there is no tomorrow. Forgive like you mean it. Forgive until there is no more hatred and spite to round the bend of hypocrisy's shadow in your wake, and you will be rewarded. Rewarded with the prize of growth for your soul, serenity for your Spirit and the understanding that there is no other way to live, for you are complete. The burdens — the holes of might — are gone. Grace and fortitude are your crowning glory, and you will be redeemed, the closer to the Angels on your journey home to God. The Angels sing; the path is cleared.

The time is now to do good deeds and put away the pettiness and loneliness of a life half lived. Don't hanker for all that glitters in a life devoid of starlight on the soul. Do your best, and you will find that the music of your soul is a sweet serenade of love for all who find you dear. This is the way, the truth and the hope of all mankind.

Liberty is at your door; the liberty of a life well lived, well served in the light of love. The liberty of Free Will calling; liberty to try and fail, then try again. The hope of a future well-regarded — a blissful tune of serenity in the dreams that carry you home. Be careful what you wish for, as the 'morrow brings another day, another test to bring you to your knees. Persevere, don't give in, and all will be well.

The means justifies the end, that is how karma plays out. Sing a song of joy for when all is said and done, the truth will astound you. For you are a child of God and nobody can deny it. The joy is in the beginning and the end, and everything in between. It is the joy of living, the joy of giving, and the joy of returning home knowing you have done your best and the future is assured.

* * *

This is the way to God's Kingdom — through the valley of darkness and onto greener pastures. Do not worry on the 'morrow ... what will be, will be. The story remains the same — the never-ending journey of your soul. Abide by me in all you say and do, and the future is assured. For I am the truth to set you free ... I am the wheel to lead your barrow ... I am. For when you come to me in goodness and in grace, I will lead you home. I will carry your burdens and the light will show the way. Hallelujah.

—Jesus

* * *

7

The Knowledge Tree of life

Patiently I wait for thee, a host of new beginnings for your soul. Are you ready for the wave that keeps on coming? Surrender to the peace, surrender to the joy — the true believers' signpost of the Ages.

—Jesus

* * *

Adam and Eve were the caretakers of their souls. They had choices to make, chances to take. They lived in love; they had colour and joy and all things bounteous. Life was peaceful, life was harmonious, and happiness was their lot; a burden to be sure. Along came the snake with a wise and clever plot — a bargain to be made — for all around the future was grand, but ennui set in. There were questions for all, and knowledge was the prize of the Ages.

What price knowledge? What price the truth of your existence? ... the essence of your being? ... the creation of the world? The light shone brightly, the rainbows illuminated the perfect state of being — all light and joy and peace for all. The snake, of course, was Lucifer the Light — all knowing, all seeing, wise beyond words, a fallen star, an ego of might, the trappings of an Angel. He wanted more, he wanted all; good deeds could not sustain him. He wanted power, he wanted might. His goal was history in the making.

A bargain was set to lose the cover of the Ages, lose the grandeur of the day, and lose the simple pleasures of a life of joy. All for knowledge, pure and simple. All for knowledge of the truth of God, the truth of creation, the truth of all.

Lucifer had this knowledge at the right-hand side of God — the co-creator in eternity, the captain of the guard. He set about his grand plot. What price for a soul? In all the honour found in mankind, this deal they could not refuse. They could not understand the full horror of what they were bargaining with. Their temerity became them, and they sold their souls for knowledge. A bargain set is not to break, and Lucifer cajoled them.

At each Age of Mankind, Lucifer is roaming still, his bargain set in blood. For all who dare to claim the prize, Lucifer is ready. The bargain thus was simple truth — to understand eternity. In return, Lucifer prowls around, his henchmen at the ready. For those who choose to hate and kill, he has a simple deal, 'Come with me, and power and glory will be yours forever more. Give me your soul and we will rule; all power and dominion'. A blackest choice, a damning ride to hell, no less, a hell of your own making. No turning back, no second chance, no time to reconsider.

God looks down, all wise and knowing, His flock all strewn around. Free Will is what He gave us then and Free Will takes us home. Follow God — it's hard to do when Lucifer is prowling, he offers power and status in a world of pain and hardship. Many souls, they pay the price, they are tempted all the while. They cannot understand Free Will; they think God has forsaken them. They look around, they see despair, they see pain and bloody wars, greed and hate, murder and rape — how to find God in this world? They fail to see that the test is thus of every human being. A test of faith, of belief in God, and to understand the nature of their being.

For all are struggling, know no doubt, to understand their God. To believe in love and live in joy is the test of every day. Lucifer knows the weakness of mankind, the greed and spite and envy. He roams arounds, he tempts with might, and the honour he is keeping. He wants the pain. He wants the evil of a world that is in turmoil. He saves full strength for the powerful elite whose temptations come at speed. Many resist, the good wins out and righteousness saves the day, but some they falter, their choices foul and they don't make the grade.

To walk the walk of the true believers is a

blessing of the Ages, a gift for the holiest of thou, a joy to behold in the playground of life. Gather ye all, for the time to deliver is upon us. It behoves the state of man to wonder why the barnacles of time keep on growing, yet no-one understands the truth of their existence. Why is wisdom held by so few? Why do so many suffer with pain and sorrow in their midst? This is the quandary of life, the missing link, the truth to ignite the passion and the glory of the one true God.

God looks on, love in His heart, He knows what rankles mankind. He knows the temptations, the tipping point, as they get lost in mire. God is wise, is merciful, His Master Plan at stake, but He knows that love will win the day as the Age begins again.

God is everywhere, my friend, and you can see it all around — the beautiful hand of God's sweet mercy. Do not forget the Ages of Man as he comes in from the wilderness, the Age of surrendering to the peace and glory of God's true Word. Many Ages have come to pass, and mankind's journey has been fraught, but here we are on the precipice and no-one can deny it.

Take what you can from history's glance, but you will find that the way to yonder glory is to relish the stars that come out to support you. Relish the Ages of Mankind that bring him home again. The best way to reach for the stars is to journey within and see what doth lie there.

See the journey of your heart and soul and open up to new beginnings. Take the journey of love and see what you are made of. Grasp the truth of your being; grasp what lies beneath the stolen summer of your soul, for you will be redeemed. Fight for glory, fight for the chance to be whole again, to forgive yourself and recover from the pain that lies there burning.

Understand the fruitfulness of your labours and the journey back to God. This is the way to deliver the prize, the prize of eternal love and redemption for your soul. This is where the journey takes you. This is the heartache of man, served raw and just for starters — the buffet of life, the journey to the edge of beyond, where no-one wants to take you lest you get lost by the wayside.

The Blue Light leads us home again in pure light and song; a song of love, of wisdom too, of joy and eternal good. This light will lead a thousand hearts to do what they deem right. A thousand sinners turned around by goodness of the light. The light will shine upon the souls of those who feel the pull. They'll understand the choice they make; they'll understand the truth.

The light is just and merciful, it calms and soothes the world. It reaches out and saves the day under harness of the Moon. The Moon, you know, is looking on in pleasure of the day. The Moon is set to take a bow and go on its merry way. The Blue Star is a star of love, of wisdom, pure and true. It sets the scene for truth and dare; truth to make all knowledge known, dare to see it through.

We know this star in memories deep, we

remember why we came here — to pass our tests, our life of pain, so we progress our souls. We awaken to the truth, the Blue Light serves, and we are all much wiser. We live in peace, forgive the rest, we wonder why we doubted. In magnanimous pride we make the grade, our futures in the planning. For those of us who refuse to accept the nature of our world, the pain is deep — denial, more so — a hunger of the soul. A hunger that is empty ache, all pain and wrath and sorrow. A hunger and a thirst for love, for meaning of the 'morrow.

The Blue Light comes around every Age — a marker of the righteousness of holy light, holy ground, holy beings. Every Age, the scene is set for mankind to get it right, to understand the truth of all, the hunger of the night. The Blue Light seeks to pave the way, to lead so we may follow.

Eternity's Rest — a bough so deep, to rest our weary sorrows. And rest we will, the light will heal, it will energise and soothe. It will awaken souls to the truth of all and cleanse away the sorrow. The pain we feel will see us through. We know not why we go there, but we know the truth is sitting still and will meet us on the 'morrow.

* * *

Once in a while — the story goes — the Line Master sang the tune. Now, of course, the tuneless go their merry way and barter with their soul.

—Jesus

8

The future is assured

All that is, I am.

—Jesus

All that is old is new again. Once again, mankind is faced with sorrow from the deep, sorrow erupting from the mire, sorrow where they found it. Locked away, it stirs anew the horror of our own making, the horror that is ours to own. Its needs are great, it finds new home, don't let it come to ground. It is the pain of many moons ago, the pain from Holy Lands. Send out love to send it on its way, for many futures come to pass as it goes round again. In dormant land it bides its time for the holiest of mankind.

Mankind knows not what's in store; they don't know why they're here. They believe in naught but selfish deeds, and money it is king. The land, of course, will expel its lot; the deeds will see the light.

They'll burst right through; the dam walls break — the blackest, blackest night. No-one will know what pain will be — what future is left there waiting — until the time is right to see the horror of their making.

This has happened long ago in the eons of your mind. You feel the stir, the fear is real. Don't feed the beast, stay true and dear and you will survive the fall. For once again, the Holy Ground is shrinking by the minute; all jackboots, guns and poison gas are waiting by the precipice. When many they will feel the pull — the need to jump or run — and over yonder we can see the innocent get slaughtered. The deeds will show mankind the way, to fathom what they've done.

* * *

The many-headed 'dragon' is set to come this way again, and you know that its legacy will keep on calling. This has been predicted in the stars. Time and time again, the truth was out there but no-one sought to join the dots and tell it how it is. Mankind will live inside a bubble until the champagne pops its cork. The fizz will take us nowhere fast; Mother Earth will see that once again she needs to keep on rolling. Round and round, she needs to clear the path that keeps on forming. She'll persevere, and we will find the world it keeps on changing. Destiny takes a swipe at how we've wronged her.

The tide will turn, the light will fade, and the

beaches turn to mud. To the hills is where to head to find the status quo. The animals all know the score; they feel it in their bones. They accept their fate with fortitude and grace, human beings not so. Families split, on the move, it is a tragic sight. Mother Earth goes cap in hand for the journey of her life.

Many, many moons ago the light was in the night-sky. Heaven sent, the moon will change — all orange, deep and foreboding. The orange, it will make a stand, will deepen all the while. The scientists they don't know the score, they blame it on the eye. Any which way you look at it, it is a miraculous sight. It gives them such a fright; they think they know the truth of it, but the truth is out there waiting. They feel the pull of golden light and many hearts are racing.

* * *

When mankind decides to do what's right, he'll come in from the cold. He'll understand the fruitfulness of living with love and light. For many, many moons have passed, and he's forgotten how to love. He's forgotten about the truth of life and sleepwalks all the while. He needs to know just what's in store when he passes to the light. To be prepared and to live in love is the only way that's right.

Jesus Christ will come again, and he'll call our names with love. He takes us by the hand and leads us to righteousness of being. When the music stops, he will be there to greet us. He will love and cherish us forever in eternity. For he is our Saviour, he is the way and the hope of mankind, the signpost to our destiny, God's messenger of love.

If you call to him, he will be ready, waiting by your side. He will soothe and protect and lead you onwards, ever upwards to the glory of your soul. For the Christ Light never fades, never dims. It is ever-present, a never-ending reminder of the key to set you free from the tyranny of life — from the pain, the sorrow, and the ache of emptiness in a materialistic world gone mad.

Jesus is the key to your redemption. Take the journey, call his name and he'll be there to greet you. In the starlight of pure surrender he will be waiting, and glory be to God.

* * *

Come to me all who seek the Holy Grail — the holy ground of love. I will honour and cherish thee and lead you to my door. For when all is said and done, the world turns and I will be there to greet you. I will mop your fevered brow and bow to your endeavours. I will comfort you and show you what you are made of — the strengths that show the way, and the curse of good intentions that assail you in the night. For here I am ... the truth that has been waiting.

—Jesus

* * *

Once in a while, the stage is set for those who care to believe, for those who see the grandeur of the day and the love for all to share. They are the true believers and will lead the day in sunshine and grace. Holy ones — share the light, do what you came to do! The day is young, and nothing will deter you. Spread your wings and fly. Over the mountaintops, eternity awaits. Be love in motion — graceful and kind, wise and loving — and nothing will defeat you. Leave all negativity behind and go forwards now with grace. Behold the season of your glory. The beauty of your intentions will come to rest upon your soul, and all of the world will be in raptures to the day that Jesus Christ came calling.

When all is said and done, the future is assured. Many a day and many a night, the stars come out to play. They see the future as it unfolds, they know the glory times ahead. They know mankind's journey through the Ages is a fait accompli, a mission of glory, a pre-determined leap of faith that no good journeyman can avoid. Look into the future as you know it. What do you see? The baggage of the soul? Or the loving, gentle kindness of a Master in disguise?

Be prepared for glory. Be prepared to be your best and the light will shine upon you like a sunbeam on the lap of time, forever holding court to love and righteousness. Go now, in peace and love and virtue, for behind you lies the test of slumber and a new beginning for your soul.

* * *

Believe in me and I will provide sustenance. I'll soothe and protect you and glory will be by your side. Come to me with all your worries and I will carry them home. For I am the light, the truth and the way of all mankind ... All that is, will be.

—Jesus

9

Conclusion

Talk to thee, pray in earnest, for what else is your heart for? Be gentle, kind and true and I will comfort thee. I give you glory, I give you love, my arms will comfort thee. In times of darkness, worry and loneliness I am always there to comfort and cherish. The price of love, of course, is never-ending joy.

Take the prize, I call to you, and you will be redeemed. God's love is just, is kind and true and He calls you to your task. Come sit awhile and we will see what holy days are looming — holy days to talk of love and educate the masses. Holy days where you will wonder, 'Why did I worry so?' It will happen, it's in the stars, you will not hang around. The words will come. Like a tunnel of love, they'll knock you to your knees, for all the world is vulnerable, they need to know the truth.

—Jesus

* * *

Believe what may, there comes a time when all must know the future that awaits them, the glory days of summer, and the fruit that ripens on the vine. Be like the Dove — strong and true — and understand the purpose of your existence and the truth of your endeavours. Carry the torch for all that is good and holy, and all that is right with the world will make it to a future that is blessed. Blessed with new beginnings, a home to be proud of — the way of the Lord to everlasting glory of the soul.

As is above, so is below — so we must act in holy demeanour. We carry our hearts on our sleeves for all to see the love that doth reside there. We think always of others, with no greed or suffering to be found. This is the holy trinity — this is the trifecta of love, joy and forgiveness to all — sweet harmony of the soul. For when we act in love, our souls will shine, and when our souls shine, we are Heaven-blessed and know not the suffering of the common man. We are holier than thou, and our deeds will carry us home. Our souls will be in rapture of the night that set us free; free to roam at last amongst the Angels of the Light. Free to leave our burdens to the Masters of vibration to transform and transmute into the magic of the day.

How about the time is now to see what you are made of? No-one knows the joy of summer until it follows them home to the frozen plains of winter. Remember all you came to do. Recall the night-sky of your intentions. Forgiveness is a rite of passage, a glorious entree to the majesty of life where those who feel God's love can never turn their back. They know the future will astound them. They know the lessons to be learned in the tests and trials along the way, tests for all believers and non-believers alike. Tests to help you make the grade and wonder why you faltered. Tests to keep you grounded, with love right by your side. This is the way to peace and prosperity of the soul.

The wicked know no other way, for theirs is a path of solitude and loneliness as all God's children seek to carry their burdens home. This is the test of love — carry or release, forgive or find that the burdens are too great as they strangle in the night. With good intentions lay them to rest, and peace will carry you home. Serenity's reach is right outside your door.

Be still and be holy. Go inside and seek the virtues of your soul. For when you are one, you are many— the many-faceted diamond of your soul. Journey to the heart of mankind and find where you belong — on the pathway to your soul. Open up, let Spirit in, and the music will surround you.

Listen now to all that comes to greet you. Understand the future as you make it. To dream the dreams of the non-believers is a sorry tale to tell; devoid of hope on the journey back to God, devoid of understanding of the burdens we all wear.

Jeopardy in motion is the wayward stance of

life; jeopardy that we've come so far and not realised our true intentions. Jeopardy that we believe money is king and power is supreme — power over others, power over material possessions — and ignorance of the true meaning of a life well lived in honour and glory and righteousness of being.

Live as you are meant to, with love and joy the mainstay of your creation. The jury master's verdict is to see what you are made of. The joy to be had from living a pure, loving and righteous life is a prize worth knowing, a life worth living. It is joy in the extreme to know that you have claimed the prize of glory for your soul, and for all the measures known to mankind, this one will take you home. Home to God, home to Heaven above, where all will find the key to their redemption.

The best way to impart this truth is to live a perfect example of love and light from this day forward. Resist the urge to be hateful or spiteful. Resist the urge to be jealous or unkind. Love like there is no tomorrow. Love like the seas will part and carry you to God's doorstep. For all along we flounder. We flounder here, we flounder there, we give a little, take a little, and we know why we stumble.

Persevere, carry on, and do not give into negativity. The day has come to lay your burdens down. The day has come to rise above the pettiness of life to see what you are made of. The naysayers will explode in rage and ridicule at all you've come to know, but ignore them, they know no other story but the pain that grips them tight and strangles in the night. They know no other way. The light dims and still they think the darkness is their friend.

When all is said and done, mankind will make the grade. They'll pass their tests as they go round again. The light will dim, but all will know the future is assured. For when the day has come that brings them to their knees, they'll understand the truth that sat there waiting. All will be known; all will be understood — the fruits of their endeavours come to rest upon their souls. The cards are marked, the truth is known, and all will be in raptures to their soul, for the learning is supreme — the eternal journey of the heart and soul as it progresses to the light.

The day has come to lay your burdens down. The day has come to journey to the heart of mankind and, saving grace, send love and forgiveness evermore. Love, light and grace to save the day — wisdom of the journey home to God that each of us must take. Wisdom of the winding path of iniquity's shadow that calls to us with might.

Come save the day and live in honour of the truth to set us free. All is forgiven.

* * *

I am the light, the truth and the way and I come to you in glory of the light, the holy light on holy ground which you seek to foster. Rein it in, the love that comes to you will bring you to your knees. For you are joy in motion, a sight to behold, a healing pair of hands, a poetry in motion. Cherish this time and don't look back. Look forwards now with love. With light to lead the way, climb the path to glory. Behold the majesty of the light ... it seeks to surround you and make you whole.

—Jesus

Epilogue

Many doubt the wisdom that is presented. Many doubt the truth of their beginnings. Stuck on the treadmill of life, many believe that, come what may, the truth will greet them on the 'morrow when they have more time to ponder.

Not so ... you need to grasp the truth with both hands. Do not dally, do not worry over pettiness and the daily grind we all must bear. Delight in all that comes your way. Do not wait by the roadside to your deliverance as the train of good fortune rushes by, wondering why you falter.

Do not delay, do not hesitate. Instead, rush in and declare, 'I am here Lord, I am ready. I am your humble servant. I am proud to serve you and honour be thy name'.

* * *

Come to me and the stars will surround you, they'll wash over you in goodness of the light. For when you see the pathway to your soul, you'll know the time is now and all will seek to lighten the load and help you on your journey to the light. For all who seek to know me know that I will not forsake them, I will journey with them to the light and lay their sorrows down. I will nourish and protect them in honour of the day their heart opened anew, and all will see the virtue that resides there. For I am the peace within … I am the signpost to your goal … the goal of everlasting joy and serenity for your soul, and I am by your side forever more. Journey within and sing a song of joy, for when the candle flame is lit, the light will reign supreme. Know this, and you know true love. Know this, and your burdens will fly away, and may you ever call my name. Hallelujah.

—Jesus